TOTAL DRAMA

COLOURING BOOK

YOUNG WRITERS GROUP

Made with ♥ on the Notion Press Platform
www.notionpress.com

Contents

Acknowledgements

Coloring is a quite entertaining activity, which sometimes serves as an anti-stress for adults who have accumulated fatigue from various circumstances, as it stimulates the brain to concentrate on a totally different exercise, thus releasing the burden, many therapists endorse this.

For this purpose, many books have been created to paint, which are quite varied, in this case we will talk about the cartoon animals for coloring, which in addition to their good drawings are a memory of our childhood.

Among the animated animals are: The Lion King, the Black Stallion, Lassie, Dumbo, Puss in Boots, the Fox and the Hound, Uncle Tiger and Uncle Rabbit, Bugs Bunny, Tom and Jerry, Wile E. Coyote and the Road Runner, Daffy Duck, etc.

CHAPTER ONE

Total Drama

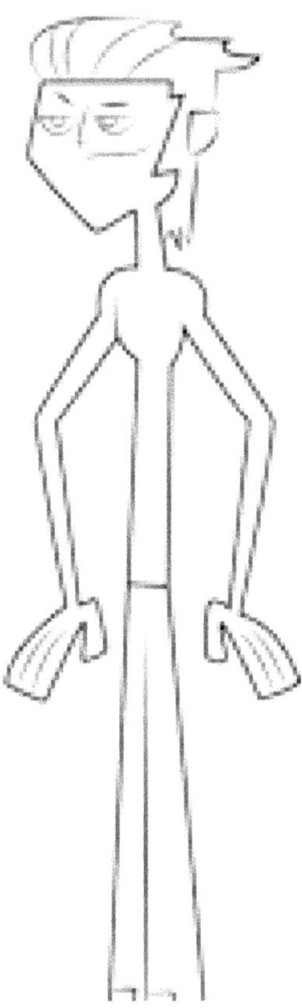

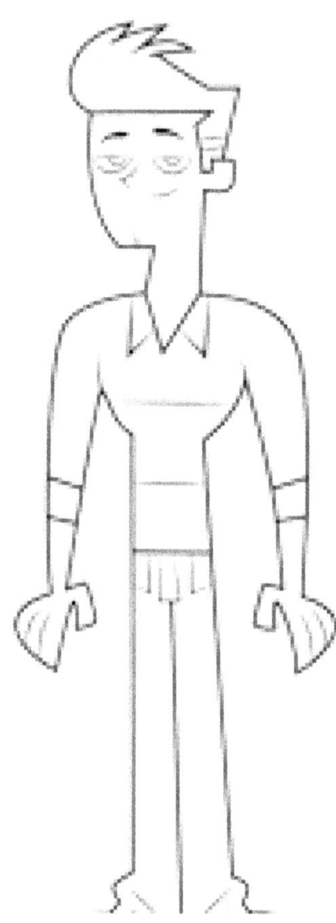

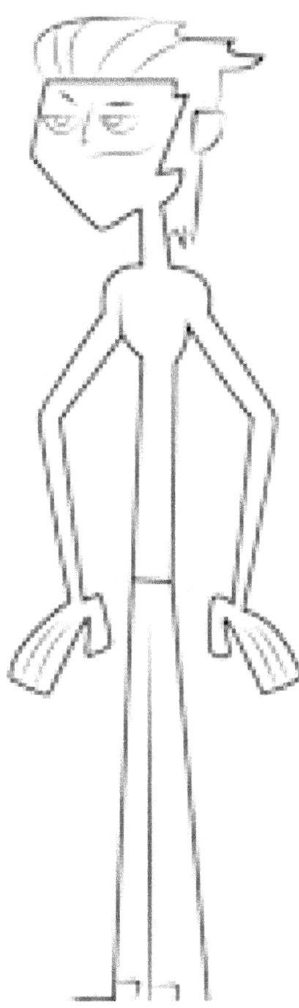

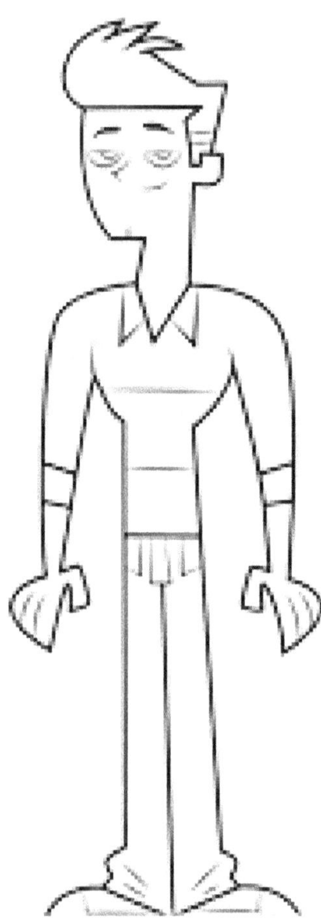

Ywg.official

Young Writers Group (YWG.OFFICIAL) is an organisation which is working to help writers in showcasing their work in front of vast number of readers . We offers a budget friendly packages to our writers. We are working as a writer's helping society. You can have a talk with us regarding publishing your book on our instagram :@YWG.OFFICIAL
Or you can drop your mail on ywg.co.in@gmail.com
Else you can also contact us on following numbers
Akash: 7404390981
Aashika: 9634644516